MW01281800

RSVP24

RSVP: The Directory of Illustration and Design is published by Richard Lebenson and Kathleen Creighton, P.O. Box 050314, Brooklyn, NY 11205. None of the artwork in this book may be reproduced in any manner without written permission from the individual artist. ©1999 Richard Lebenson. All rights reserved 1999, Volume 24, number 1. ISBN 1-878118-08-0. Printed in China.

RSVP24

www.rsvpdirectory.com
info@rsvpdirectory.com

CREDITS

Publishers Richard Lebenson and Kathleen Creighton **Coordination/ Sales** Richard Lebenson **Design and Promotion** Kathleen Creighton, Michael Kelly **Business and Promotion** Joe Greenstein **Office Manager** Harvey Wilson **Sales** Paul Krauss **Traffic/Sales** Frank Attong **Cover Illustration** C F Payne **Cover Design** Jim Wilmink **Website Design** James Spahr **Typesetting** Stephen Bodkin **Thanks To** Ken Chung, Tom Chung, Kathy Copas, George Dick **Prepress** Everbest/China **Printing** Four Color Imports LTD and Everbest/China

Contents

RSVP24 features the work of 243 artists, illustrators and designers nationwide, indexed alphabetically by specific skills and by region in our geographic index. RSVP Callback® 718 857 9267, is our around the clock answering service. (See page 304 for complete details.)

COVER DESIGNER

Jim Wilmink

RSVP 24

Born in Cincinnati, Ohio, **Jim Wilmink** is a graduate of the Art Academy of Cincinnati. Jim is a principal and graphic designer at the firm Design Associates, which opened its doors in 1994. His design experience includes several years with Williams McBride Design in Lexington, Kentucky. Jim's clients represent a variety of companies and services, and have included such firms as IBM, Sunoco/Kocolene Oil, Kentucky Utilities and Memorial Hospital of Seymour. Jim's design work has been recognized in major national and international communications art exhibits and publications, and has received numerous awards over the years.

He currently lives in Cincinnati with his wife, Amy, and their two daughters, Olivia and Gabrielle.

C F Payne

24
RSVP

COVER ILLUSTRATOR

C.F. Payne is a freelance illustrator based in his hometown of Cincinnati, Ohio. He is a 1976 graduate of Miami University and the Illustrator's Workshop under the tutelage of Alan Cober, Mark English, Bernie Fuchs, Bob Peak, Fred Otnes and Bob Heindel. After brief studio stints in Akron, Ohio and Chicago, Illinois he began his freelance career in Dallas, Texas in national publications. Time Magazine, Esquire, GQ, Sports Illustrated, Money Magazine, MAD, Penthouse, The New York Times, and the New Yorker to name a few.

Over the past few years his work has received national recognition by such publications as Communications Arts, Step-by-Step, Society of Publication Designers, American Illustration, Society of Illustrators of New York, and the Society of Illustrators of Los Angeles. His work has received Gold and Silver Medals and the Hamilton King Award from the Society of Illustrators of New York. From September of 1996 until January of 1997 his work was honored with an exhibition of some thirty original illustrations at the Cincinnati Art Museum.

Over the years he has lectured extensively, juried numerous shows and taught at the college level. In 1996 he was president of the Art Directors Club of Cincinnati and Chairman of the 38th Society of Illustrators Annual Competition.

He currently resides in Cincinnati with his wife Paula and children, Trevor 13, and Evan 7.

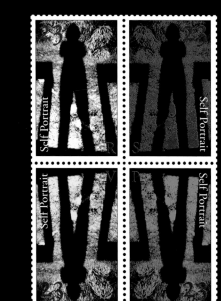

RSVP's Self-Portrait Competition

Over the centuries self-portraits have understandably been one of the great artistic preoccupations. We were pleased to choose it as the theme for our fourth annual national competition. A total of 736 entries were received, and one point was absolutely proven: The creative act comes in an amazing variety of sizes, colors and stylistic impulses.

Jurors
Marshall Arisman, Illustrator
Richard Berenson, Designer
David Levine, Illustrator
Jackie Merri Meyer, V.P. Creative Director, Warner Books

First Prize *full-color reproduction plus $1000.*
Harvey Dinnerstein

Second Prize *full-color reproduction plus $500.*
Felicia Arikawa

Third Prize *full-color reproduction plus $250.*
Daniel Adel

Our gallery section features entries by the finalists and semi-finalists.

The next competition being sponsored by RSVP (View from the Edge) has a deadline of June 30, 1999. For complete information, see pages 34-39.

First Place

Harvey Dinnerstein 718.783.6879

Harvey Dinnerstein was born in Brooklyn, NY in 1928. He attended the Art Students League in New York City and the Tyler Art School of Temple University in Philadelphia. His education included two years of study with Moses Soyer.

Listed among Dinnerstein's many achievements are seventeen solo exhibitions, including a 1994 retrospective at the Butler Institute of Art in Youngstown, Ohio. He is represented in many major collections, most notably the National Museum of Art in Washington DC, and the Metropolitan and Whitney museums in New York City.

Dinnerstein has also received a host of awards and has a long list of published works to his credit.

Third Place

Daniel Adel 212.989.6114

Second Place

Felicia Arikawa 415.661.8613

Gallery

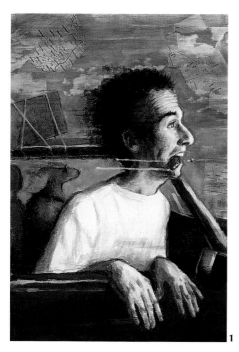

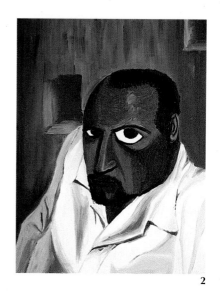

1 Chad Cameron 415.861.2833 **2** Travis K Schuerman 914.238.0311 **3** Johanna St Clair 415.386.8605

4

5

6

7

8

9

4 Rudy Gutierrez 212.568.2848 **5** Rachel Roberts 617.441.3992 **6** Ingo Fast 718.387.9570
7 Philip Straub 203.261.4334 **8** Bill James 305.238.5709 **9** Kenneth Francis Dewey 607.639.2543

10

11

12

13

14

15

10 Gregory A Sand 212.475.2681 **11** Craig Larotonda 415.551.1023 **12** David Ricceri 718.852.8987
13 Joel Edwards 212.979.0656 **14** Mark Garro 203.661.6922 **15** Chang Park 718.651.3764

16

17

18

19

20

21

16 Rocco J Mirro 516.355.0675 **17** Igor Tiul'panoff 973.325.5164 **18** Alison Zawacki 916.368.7157
19 Brooks Burgan 909.464.5423 **20** Emily Thompson 212.245.2543 **21** Jean Hunter 718.898.1308

22

23

24

25

26

27

22 David Choe 213.549.9161 **23** Linda S Wingerter 860.434.7977 **24** Bob Pepper 718.875.3236
25 Tom Nick Cocotos 212.620.7556 **26** Greg Swearingen 1.800.210.8236.02
27 Christopher Buzelli 877.614.8111

28

I am GReat

HAPPY BIRTH DAY

29

VALERIE ✦ SOKOLOVA

30

31

33

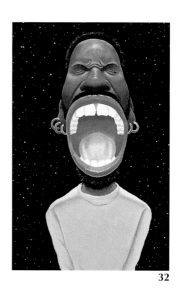

32

28 Thomas Reis 718.596.4548   **29** Kazz Ishihara 212.964.9895   **30** Valerie Sokolova 718.891.0894
31 Brian Cognazzo 410.882.1777   **32** Vern Edwards 404.373.6495   **33** Sandra Filippucci 860.927.1101

34

35

36

37

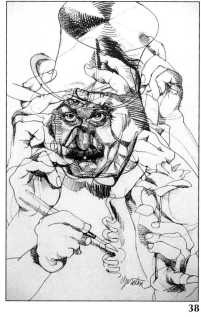

38

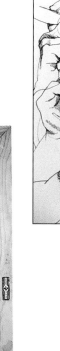

39

34 David Levinson 973.614.1627 **35** Ethan Sand 212.475.2681 **36** Dugald Stermer 415.777.0110
37 Carl Johnson 941.362.7326 **38** Gerry Gersten 212.752.8490 **39** Lori Nelson Field 973.783.1321

41

42

43

44

45

40 Victor Stabin 212.243.7688 **41** Yvonne Buchanan 718.783.6682 **42** Andy Park 818.819.1116
43 Daisuke Tsutsumi 415.922.8507 **44** David Hollenbach 718.596.3888
45 Frederique Bertrand 212.535.0438

Call for entries

On the threshold of the 21st
Century, in the midst of a
digital revolution, in a world
that's filled with promise and
problems—we have chosen a
competition theme that gives
free reign to fantasy and
pushes style, medium and
content to their outer limits.
The interpretation is yours,
but the theme is *View from the Edge*

DEADLINE 6.30.99

View From the Edge

Who's Eligible Illustrators, Designers, Art Directors, Fine Artists, Students

Format for Entries 35mm slides, Chromes 4"x5" or larger; Laserprints; Iris, Fiery or Fujix Prints. All entries must be labeled with artist's name at top front. Not eligible: Work on disk; Original Art.

Entry Fee $20 for the first entry; $10 for each additional entry.

Prizes
First Place: Four-page, full-color portfolio of your work reproduced in RSVP's 25th Anniversary Edition, including 1,000 card-stock reprints for your own promotional use, plus $1,000.
Second Place: Two-page, full-color portfolio of your work reproduced in RSVP's 25th Anniversary Edition, including 1,000 card-stock reprints for your own promotional use, plus $500.
Third Place: Two-page, full-color portfolio of your work reproduced in RSVP's 25th Anniversary Edition, including 1,000 card-stock reprints for your own promotional use, plus $250.
In addition, the winners and (up to) 97 finalists will be invited to show the original art of their entries in RSVP's exhibition View from the Edge at New York's Society of Illustrators next spring.

Judges are Illustrators:
Frances Jetter, Peter Kuper, Scott Menchin, Chris Spollen

How to enter Send your entry plus check or money order (payable to RSVP) to: RSVP24 Competition, P.O. Box 050314, Brooklyn NY 11205. Also be sure to include your name, address and phone number. Those wishing their entries returned must include a stamped, self-addressed envelope.

The Fine Print: Work can be pre-existing or specially created. Artwork must not violate any copyright. Decision of the judges is final. We reserve the right to reject any entry not completed to the above specifications. We take the greatest care with all submissions, but cannot be held responsible for their safe handling or return. Do not use metered stamps on your return envelope, as our post office will not accept them. Winning entries will be used in RSVP and for promotion of the competition (with full credit to the artist). Actual artwork remains the artist's property. Multiple prizes will not be awarded to one individual.

Questions? 718.857.9267

ILLUSTRATION

JOEL SPECTOR

Barbara Garrison

12 EAST 87TH STREET, NEW YORK, N.Y. 10128
(212) 348-6382, RSVP CALLBACK ANSWERING SERVICE (718) 857-9267

305 . 576 . 8040

2045 N.W. 1st Ave.
Miami, FL 33127

michael j
RUSSO
&co
associates

DAVID MILLER

Represented BY WANDA NOWAK ph 212·535·0438 fx 212·535·1624

harrietregina marion

95 avenue B 4th floor
new york, ny. 10009
(212)475-7410, fax(212)375-9027

Tate Nation
843·884·9911

CLIFFORD FAUST

NEW YORK CITY (212) 581-9461
RSVP CALLBACK ANSWERING SERVICE (718) 857-9267

Thomas Reis

15 Douglass Street #3
Brooklyn, NY 11231
718 • 596 • 4548

The Chase Manhattan Bank • Lichter Pharma U.S. • Barbara Foods • Imagine Foods
The American Advertising Federation • Lucky Supermarkets • Chase Vista Funds

BOB • PEPPER

157 CLINTON ST., BROOKLYN HEIGHTS, NY 11201
TEL: (718) 875-3236

K A D I R N E L S O N

http://home.earthlink.net/~mikecressy/
e-mail:
mikecressy @ earthlink.net

MIKE

CRESSY

ILLUSTRATION

425•603•9669

P.O.Box 762, Issaquah, Wa. 98006

RSVP 22: Page-108, RSVP 23: Page-125

MARK FREDRICKSON

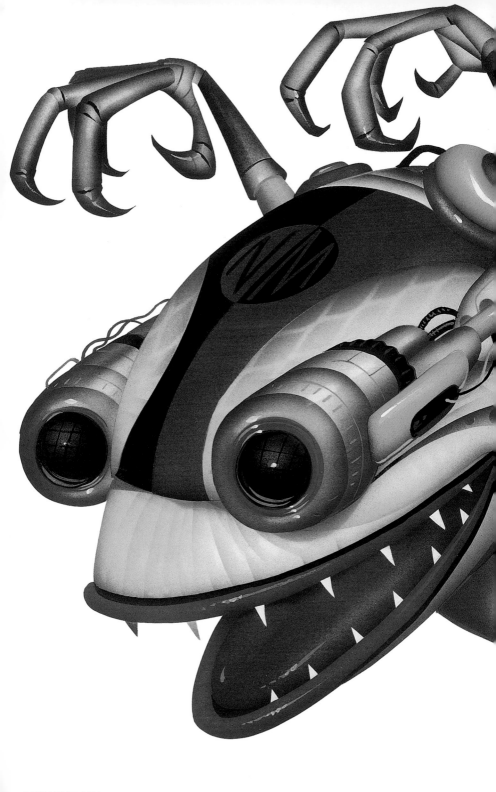

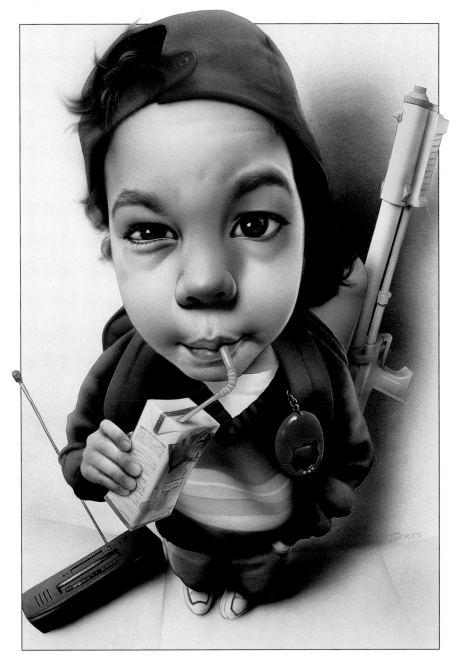

CARLOS
TORRES
716 · 695 · 9440

416-698-3304

Adam Gordon

Digital Illustration **212-532-0773** AandSand8@aol.com

DAVID·G· KLEIN

408-7TH-ST BROOKLYN-NY 11215 (718) 788-1818

Cameron Eagle

Studio: (405) 525-6676   Fax: (405) 525-7384

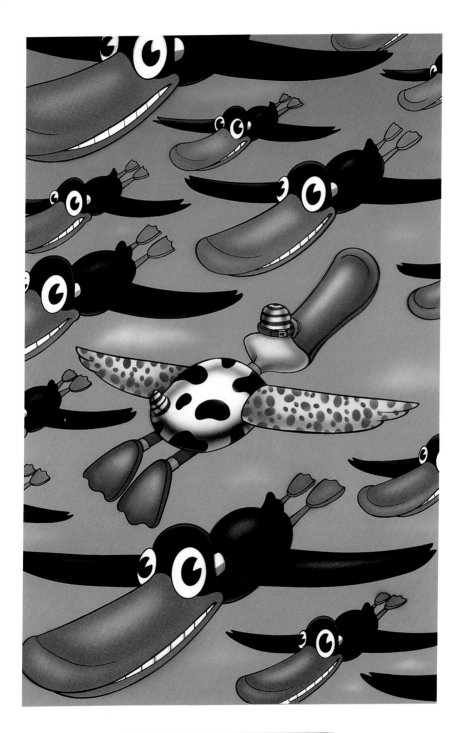

Cameron Eagle

Studio: (405) 525-6676   Fax: (405) 525-7384

ILLUSTRATION

JANET HAMLIN
TEL: (718) 768-3647   FAX: (718) 768-3675

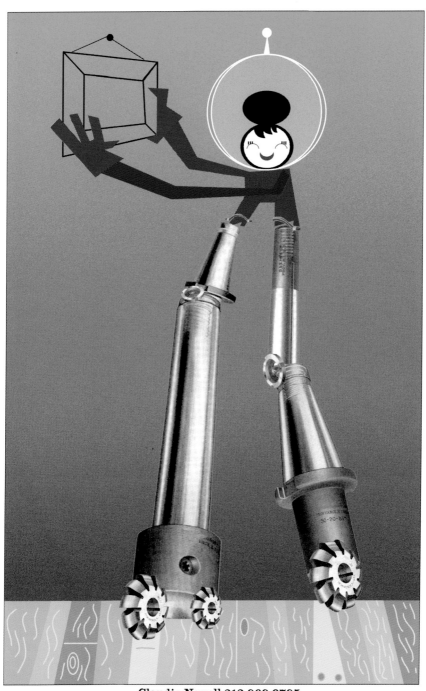

Claudia Newell 212.969.0795
http://www.mindspring.com/~cnewell
computer-assisted and free-standing illustrations.

JIM SMOLA

ILLUSTRATION 94 MAPLE HILL AVE., NEWINGTON, CT 06111 (860) 665-0305

yvonne buchanan

vox:718-783-6682   fax:718-622-4094
www.yvonnebuchanan.com

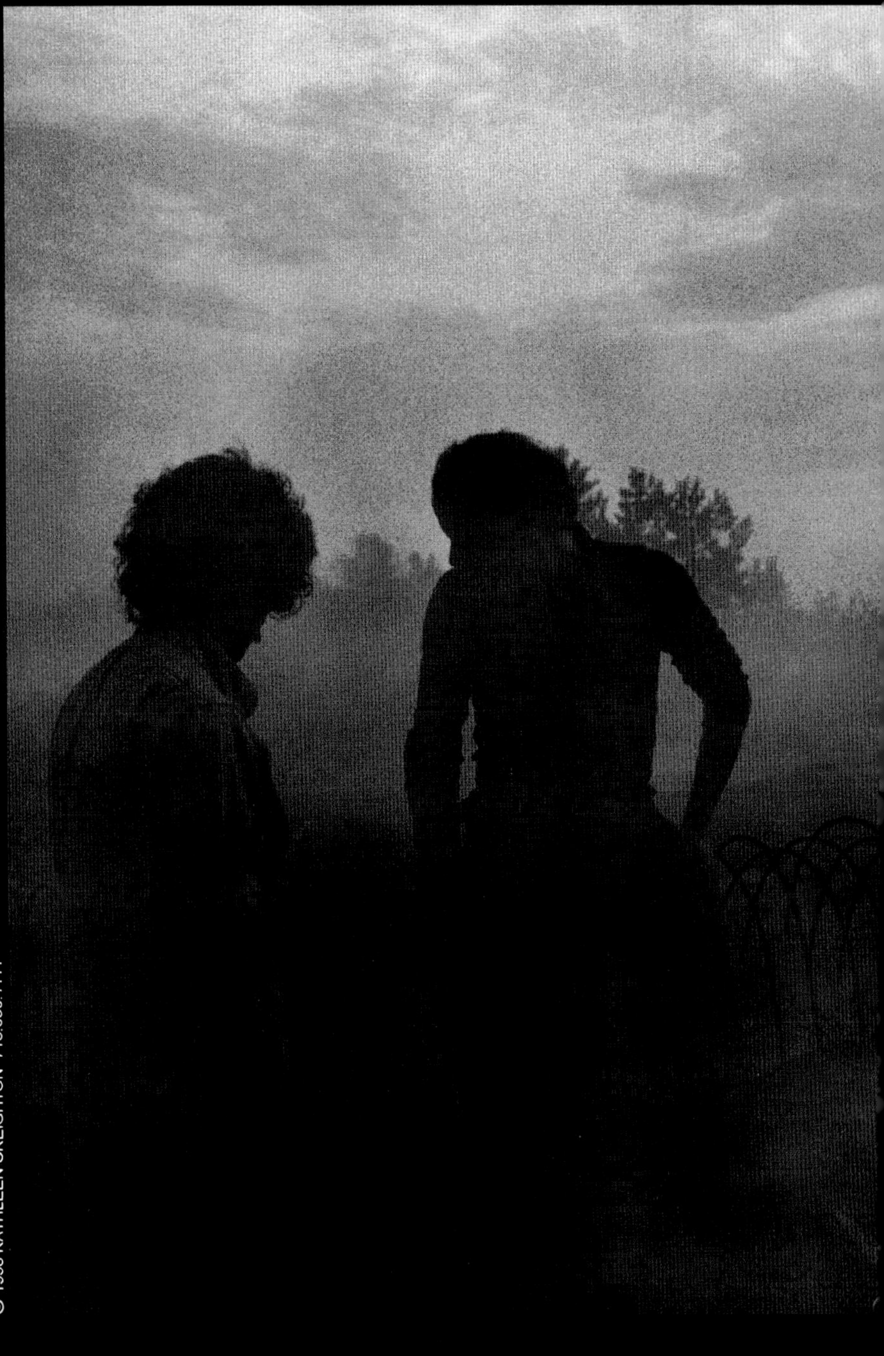

BRUCE WALDMAN

18 WESTBROOK ROAD, WESTFIELD, NJ 07090
(908) 232-2840, RSVP CALLBACK ANSWERING SERVICE (718) 857-9267

Levinson

illustration

David Levinson • 86 Parson Road Apt#2 • Clifton • NJ 07012
Telephone • Fax (973)614-1627

• CHRISTOPHER NICK •

405-943-5245 • www.cyberhall.com/nick
4305 N.W. 16th Street • Oklahoma City, OK 73107

DANIEL ABRAHAM
718·499·4006

L M POLLACK   THE MEETING

LOU M. POLLACK

Studio: **888.448.2568** or call: 718. 857. 9267

View more. b/w Portfolio, too. visit **WWW.STOCKART.COM**

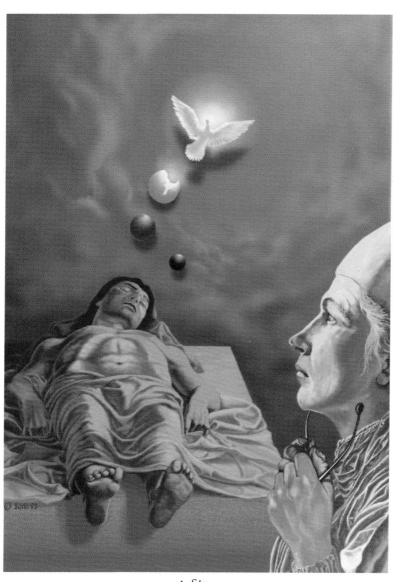

17577 Whitney Road Strongsville Ohio 44136

Sorin M. Bulucianu

Phone:(440) 891-0934

JOHN GAMPERT

Illustration/Design
718 441-2321

TIM REILLY • 407 • 860 • 7725

R
O
B
E
R
T

R
O
P
E
R

RSVP CALLBACK ANSWERING SERVICE (718) 857–9267

ROBERT ROPER

RSVP CALLBACK ANSWERING SERVICE (718) 857-9267

SIMEONE

Lauren E. Simeone
Illustrations, Inc.
855 Windsor-Perrineville Rd.
Hightstown, NJ 08520
Phone: (609) 426-4490
FAX: (609) 426-4772

CLAUDE MARTINOT

145 2nd Avenue #20 New York NY 10003 (212) 473-3137
STUDIO: 1133 Broadway #1614 New York NY 10010 (212) 229-2249
FAX:(212) 691-3657

oils on linen by

Neil Waldman

54 Rockinchair Road   White Plains, New York 10607
(914) 949-5257

PAUL YALOWITZ

RSVP CALLBACK ANSWERING SERVICE (718) 857-9267

RICHARD SOLOMON
ARTIST REPRESENTATIVE

RICHARD SOLOMON
ARTIST REPRESENTATIVE

21 MADISON AVE NYC 10016 (212) 683-1362 FAX: (212) 683-1919

Bergstein

David Bergstein / Illustration
219 Westchester Avenue
Port Chester, NY 10573
800-519-8220 • 914-935-9314
email:bcreative@mindspring.com

Curiouser & CURIOUSER!

Moderno-medieval Madness!
Miniatures & Quirky Calligraphy by
Leah Palmer PREISS 919·833·8443
fax: 919·833·8959
e: Curiouser@mindspring.com

GEORGE THOMPSON

433 WEST 43RD STREET #3E NYC 10036
PHONE & FAX 212.245.2543
RSVP CALLBACK ANSWERING SERVICE 718.857.9267

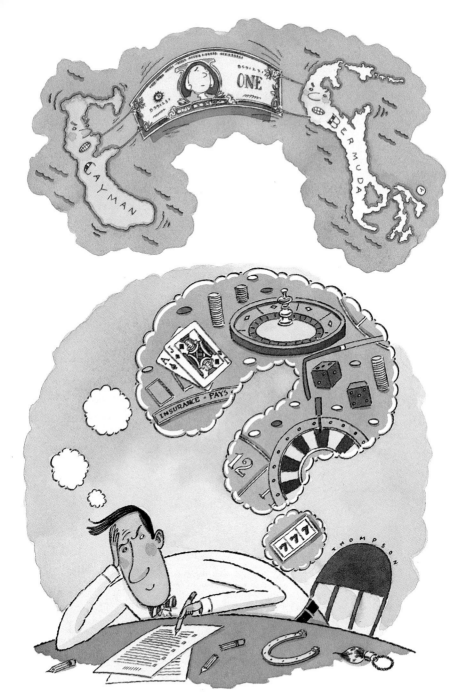

GEORGE THOMPSON

433 WEST 43RD STREET #3E NYC 10036
PHONE & FAX 212.245.2543
RSVP CALLBACK ANSWERING SERVICE 718.857.9267

©1998
Erin Marie Mauterer
Ocean, NJ 07712

1 800 258-9287
Visit www.EMauterer.com

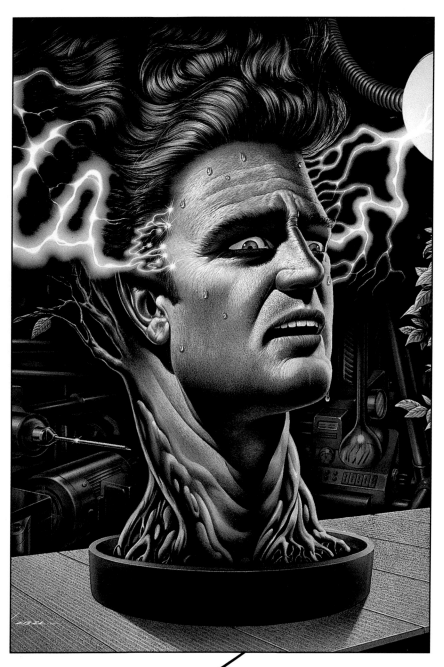

ALEX EBEL

30 NEWPORT ROAD, YONKERS, NEW YORK 10710 (914) 961-4058

Keri Lee Marino
ILLUSTRATION
212-779-3541
RSVP CALLBACK: 718.857.9267

SUSAN FOX
phone: 707-443-1427
fax: 707-442-9342
e-mail: sfox@dcta.com

Jeannie Winston

Phone/Fax 310 837 8666

BB SAMS
HUMOROUS ILLUSTRATION
(770) 464-2956

SAMSON
(516) 472-1093

BLEU TURRELL

RSVP CALLBACK 718·857·9267

TEL 312.573.1370   FAX 312.573.1445

JOEL HARLIB ASSOCIATES

INGO FAST

718 · 387 9570

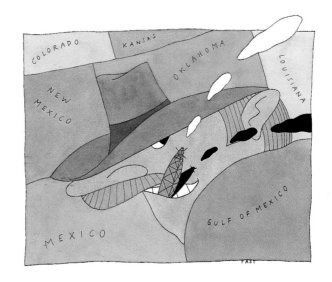

INGO FAST

718 · 387 9570

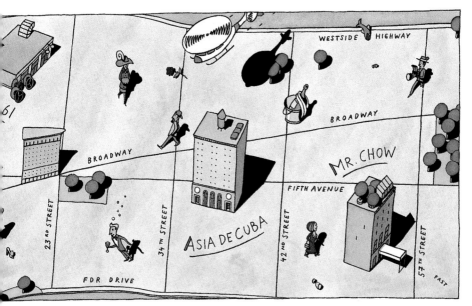

Kristine Ream
FOOD • PRODUCT • CHILDREN'S ILLUSTRATION
(412) 531-9487

.B.WHITEHEAD ⁝ ILLUSTRATION

311 Almshouse Road Doylestown, PA. 18901 215-230-7412
Fax. 215-230-7516   e-mail: sbwhitehead@nni.com

Clients: TIME, Newsweek, Sports Illustrated, SI For Kids,
Reader's Digest, TV Guide, Golf, New York Times,
Chicago Tribune, Boston Globe, AT&T, Entertainment
Weekly, Barron's, Wall Street Journal, Swing, Premiere.

Janet Hyun

Tel: 213-380-6704   Fax: 213-383-8683
RSVP Callback Answering Service.   718-857-9267

Caricatures by Ellen

Ellen M. Zucker
(215) 722-2453
emzucker@netreach.net

TOMISLAV KORDIC
516.724.8406

CECILY LANG

336 WEST END AVENUE ◆ NEW YORK, NY 10023
TEL: (212) 580-3424 ◆ FAX: (212) 580-8526
RSVP CALLBACK AVAILABLE: (718) 857-9267

DAVID RICCERI

505 COURT STREET, APT. 4H, BROOKLYN, N.Y. 11231
(718) 852-8987

STEPHEN HARRINGTON

255 WILTON ROAD WEST · RIDGEFIELD · CT · 06877
(203) 431 · 5854
REPRESENTED BY JOHN BREWSTER CREATIVE SERVICES
(203) 226 · 4724

E M I L Y   T H O M P S O N

433 West 43rd Street #3E NYC 10036
Phone & Fax 212.245.2543
RSVP Callback answering service 718.857.9267

BELGIN WEDMAN

phone (818) 707-2165   fax (818) 707-7120

Peter Pagano

Studio (908) 464-4649 · RSVP CallBack (718) 857-9267
E-mail: pjpagano@att.net

MITCHELL HEINZE
721 E MAXWELL LANE
LATHROP CA 95330
209 • 858 • 1131

JOHN STEVEN GURNEY

168 WESTERN AVENUE, BRATTLEBORO, VERMONT 05301
(802) 258-2654 FAX (802) 258-9154 RSVP (718) 857-9267

ViCKY RUBiN

(212)971-1031•RSVP Callback (718)857-9267
E-mail: Kartoonia@aol.com

John J. Crockett

(203)740-2036

RSVP Callback Answering Service (718)857-9267

Bart Rivers
ILLUSTRATION
(317)272-0632

A N N   N E U M A N N

Illustration

T: 201.**653.8927**

F: 201.**653.3092**

1101 Grand Street
Hoboken, NJ 07030

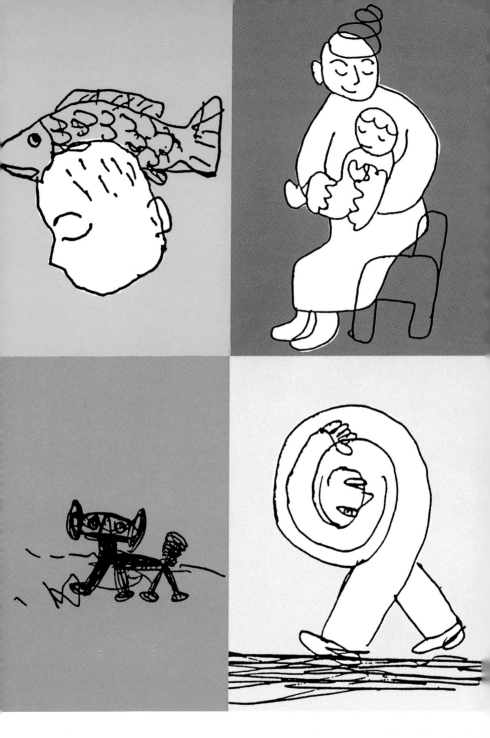

YASUO TANAKA

(718) 857-9267

1306 NW HOYT #203
PORTLAND
OREGON • 97209
503-248-0510
FAX-248-0245
email : gary@voodoocatbox.com

DAGMAR FEHLAU 5I8.962.2348

A L A I Y O   B R A D S H A W

ALANI
REPRESENTS
212 465 3355

GREGORY HERGERT

RSVP CALLBACK ANSWERING SERVICE (718) 857-9267

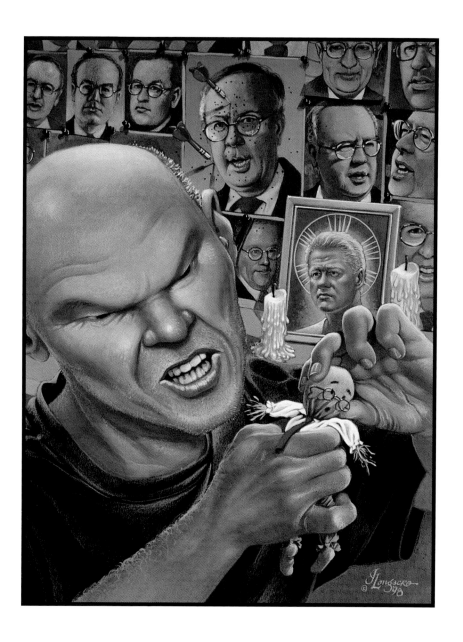

Jimmy Longacre

LONGACRE ART STUDIO
512.288.7477

On line portfolio
www.adwizards.com/longacre

ROGER HUYSSEN
54 Old Post Road
Southport, CT 06490
(203) 256·9192

©KFC/Kentucky Fried Chicken
New Colonel Sanders Character

Karen Leon

Illustration   Cartoons   Caricatures   Storyboards
154-01 Barclay Avenue • Flushing, NY 11355
718-461-2050 • 718-463-3159 • Fax Available

SUE & MARK CARLSON

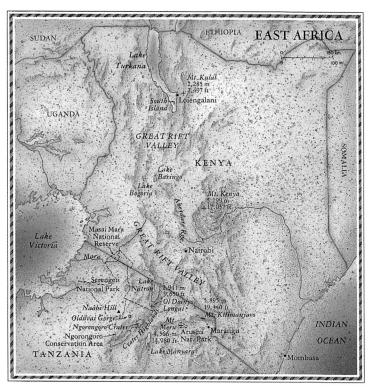

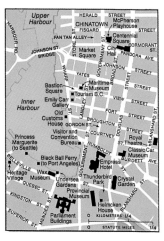

Computer maps and stock illustration available

609·971·6828

R. MARTIN

RICHARD MARTIN • 13 WALTUMA AVE., EDISON, NJ 08837 • (732) 738-4838
RSVP CALLBACK ANSWERING SERVICE (718) 857-9267

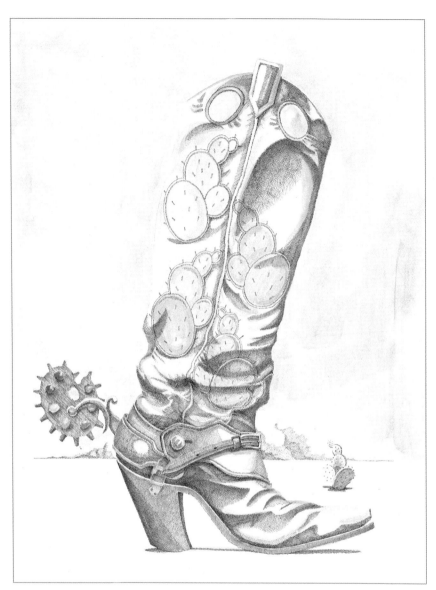

LUCINDA LEVINE
ILLUSTRATOR
301.562.9191 FAX:301.562.9199

MARK GARRO   20 KENT PLACE, COS COB, CT. 06807
(203) 661-6922   (718) 857-9267

DIGITAL
ILLUSTRATION

JERRY GONZALEZ
PHONE/FAX (718) 204-8762

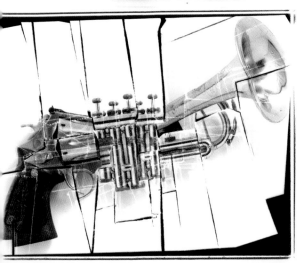

CLAY PATRICK McBRIDE

212 **989.2712**

•

FOTO-ILLUSTRATION

139

FELIPE GALINDO

Tel (212) 864-6648   Fax (212) 316-1645
email: galindo-arroyo@worldnet.att.net

STEVE HENRY, 7 PARK AVENUE, NEW YORK, N.Y. 10016 (212) 532-2487

BOOK COVERS

LARGE ILLUSTRATIONS

SPOTS

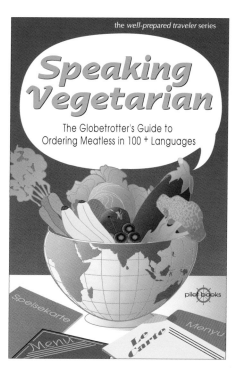

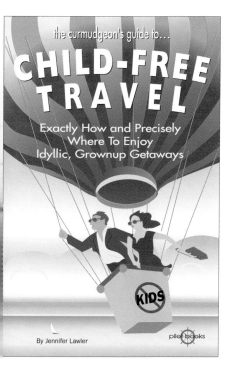

MOFFITT CECIL

AFFORDABLE COMPUTER ILLUSTRATION:
FROM FIRST CONCEPT TO FINAL PRINT

14 W. 85TH STREET•NEW YORK, NY-10024
PHONE/FAX 212-580-5320•RSVP 24 HOUR
CALLBACK SERVICE 718-857-9267

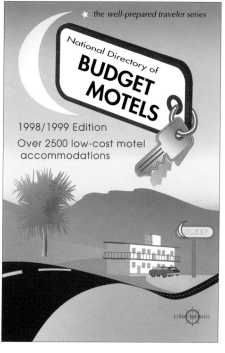

Stones from the River

-illustration-
Laurie & Zoe Studio - RSVP - (718) 857-9267

Lane du Pont   (203) 222 1562
20 Evergreen Ave. Westport, Ct. 06880
f~ (203) 222 0080 **e~** lndpnt@ct1.nai.net

LINDA WARNER ILLUSTRATION
28 Sherman Drive, Hilton Head, SC 29928
843.689.5044 • Fax 843.689.2509
E-mail address: Lindaart@rhsnet.com

CINDY SASS *ILLUSTRATION*
15 Torne Road, Sloatsburg, NY 10974
914.753.5119 *fax 914.753.5411*

Save Goldie * Call Tuko

1-800-208-2456

Tuko Fujisaki Illustraion

BARBARA GRIFFEL

ILLUSTRATION; FASHION AND BEAUTY ILLUSTRATION   (718) 631-1753

melissa iwai

Christina A. Tugeau   203•438•7307

Meryl Treatner

Christina A. Tugeau   203•438•7307

Christina A. Tugeau   203•438•7307

Christina A. Tugeau 203•438•7307

TERI SLOAT

Christina A. Tugeau   203•438•7307

Susan Simon

Christina A. Tugeau   203•438•7307

Frank Sofo

Christina A. Tugeau 203•438•7307

MACY'S
SANTALAND

Naomi Howland

Christina A. Tugeau   203•438•7307

Christina A. Tugeau   203•438•7307

PATRICK KELLEY

1040 Veto St. N.W.
Grand Rapids, MI 49504
Tel/Fax 616•458•5925

CAROLYN WATSON DUBISCH
Fantastic Visions Studio
(914) 626-4386

15 SIEBER RD. KERHONKSON, NY 12446

MICHAEL DUBISCH
Fantastic Visions Studio
(914) 626-4386
15 SIEBER RD. KERHONKSON, NY 12446

ILLUSTRATION (718) 834-6276 (718) 776-6311

Phone/Fax (718)941-3532

STEVE
SMALL
WOOD   616 249 2845

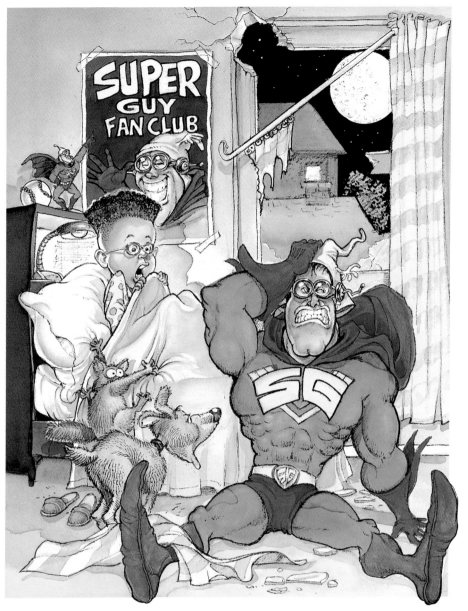

B.K. TAYLOR

24940 S. CROMWELL, FRANKLIN, MI 48025 (248) 626-8698 FAX (248) 855-8247
- CHILDREN'S ILLUSTRATION CONTACT MELISSA TURK (914) 368-8606
- EDITORIAL CONTACT IVY LEAGUE OF ARTISTS (212) 243-1333

Janice Skivington

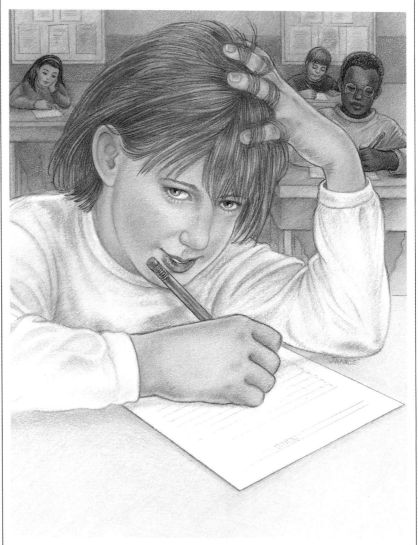

ARTISTS' REPRESENTATIVE

· GWEN WALTERS ·

50 Fuller Brook Road • Wellesley, MA 02482

TEL 781·235·8658   FAX 781·235·8635

e-mail: ArtIncGW@aol.com

Judith Pfeiffer

ARTISTS REPRESENTATIVE

· GWEN WALTERS ·

50 Fuller Brook Road • Wellesley, MA 02482

TEL 781·235·8658   FAX 781·235·8635

e-mail: ArtIncGW@aol.com

Jack Hornady Illustration
ph 202.328.1504   fx 202.387.8604

DAVID BRION
203-531-9381

JOHN JOE BRENNAN
1-203-329-8604
STAMFORD, CT.

BARRY FITZGERALD 785 841 2983

Christine Kempf
Illustrator

RSVP Callback Answering Service (718)857-9267

Jennifer DiRubbio
ILLUSTRATION

19 Prairie Lane Levittown, New York 11756.2524
phone 516.579.1872 fax

KATIE LEE

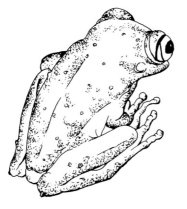

34 BITTERSWEET
SOUTH SALEM, NY 10590

PHONE AND FAX: 914•533•6237
EMAIL: katilee@aol.com

DANNY FILIPPONE

ILLUSTRATOR

Tel:(201)943-9021
Fax:(201)943-9021*51

Karol
Kaminski

ILLUSTRATION & DESIGN
330-225-8195

LAURA FREEMAN

1641 Third Avenue #29C, NYC,10128
Phone 212-423-0091 Fax 212-996-5478
http://home.att.net/~freemanhines
RSVP CALLBACK ANSWERING SERVICE 718-857-9267

LESLIE GIGNILLIAT-DAY
DIGITAL ART • PHOTO ILLUSTRATION
57 EAST 11TH ST., 9TH FLOOR, NYC, NY 10003
212.822.8882

WENDY SMITH

KEVIN
O'MALLEY

THE ARTIST NETWORK

phone **(914) 368-8606** / 9 babbling brook lane / suffern, new york 10901

DREW·BROOK·CORMACK ASSOC.

KA BOTZIS

Melissa Turk
THE ARTIST NETWORK

phone **(914) 368-8606** / 9 babbling brook lane / suffern, new york 10901

NEECY TWINEM

Melissa Turk
THE ARTIST NETWORK

phone (914) 368-8606 / 9 babbling brook lane / suffern, new york 10901
www.illustrators.net/Twinem

Karl Gude
(203) 853-1422   email: kgude@aol.com

John N Mathias
illustration 718·788·2133
520 2nd st. 3f Brooklyn, NY 11215
RSVP Callback: 718·857·9267

LAUREN KLEMENTZ-HARTE

PO Box 4006, Meriden, CT 06450
(203)235-6145

(401) 232-0105 (fax)232-9342

260 George Waterman Rd. Johnston, R.I. 02919

NANCY RODDEN

843-849-6473

ESCALMEL
COMPUTER ILLUSTRATION

ILLUSION 514·990·2029

GALLOWITZ

MALÉPART

ILLUSION   LꞀ   514·990·2029

PIFKO

ILLUSION 514·990·2029

BARROUX

ILLUSION 514·990·2029

DON DYEN

REPRESENTED BY AVERIL S. SMITH

200 S. ROBERTS ROAD #F6, BRYN MAWR, PA 19010
PHONE: (610) 520-3470 • FAX: (610) 520-3475

LANE YERKES

REPRESENTED BY AVERIL S. SMITH

200 S. ROBERTS ROAD #F6, BRYN MAWR, PA 19010

PHONE: (610) 520-3470 • FAX: (610) 520-3475

DENISE CAVALIERI FIKE

REPRESENTED BY AVERIL S. SMITH

200 S. ROBERTS ROAD #F6, BRYN MAWR, PA 19010
PHONE: (610) 520-3470 • FAX: (610) 520-3475

JOHN HOLDER

REPRESENTED BY AVERIL S. SMITH

200 S. ROBERTS ROAD #F6, BRYN MAWR, PA 19010
PHONE: (610) 520-3470 • FAX: (610) 520-3475

© LORETTA LUSTIG

Loretta Lustig

REPRESENTED BY CAROL BANCROFT FRIENDS (800) 720-7020

Higgins Bond

REPRESENTED BY **CAROL BANCROFT & FRIENDS** (800) 720-7020

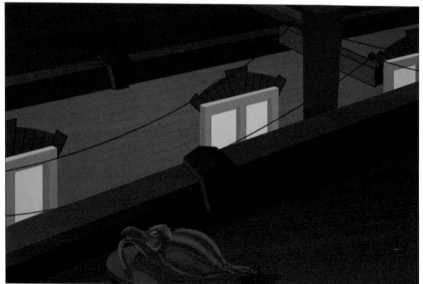

Bob & Susan Buccella

REPRESENTED BY (800) 720-7020

R. BERNAL

REPRESENTED BY (800) 720-7020

HUERTA

REPRESENTED BY **CAROL BANCROFT & FRIENDS** (800) 720-7020

Barry Rockwell

REPRESENTED BY **CAROL BANCROFT & FRIENDS** (800) 720-7020

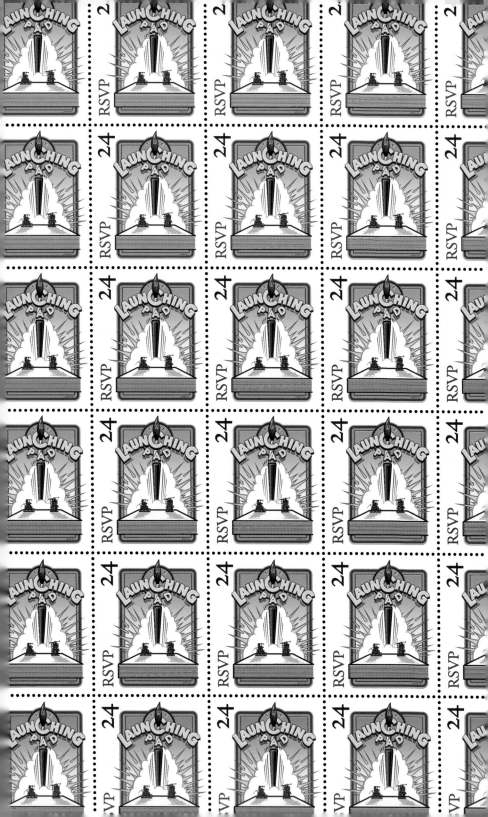

THE LAUNCHING PAD

THE LAUNCHING PAD

In two short years The Launching Pad has become one of the most exciting and highly anticipated features of our book.

RSVP has a tradition of recognizing the new, the gifted and the promising and now we've dedicated this special section to it.

The Launching Pad spotlights a select group of remarkable young illustrators, often introducing their work to the marketplace for the first time.

Included in this talented group is Nicolas Uribe Benninghoff, the winner of our annual Publication Award in the Society of Illustrator's Student Competition. His work can be seen on pages 214 and 215.

vinay ganapathy can be reached at: vinayganapathy@hotmail.com
6 manor road newmilford, connecticut 06776 (860)355-4581 or
rsvp callback answering service at (718)857-9267

Annie Lennox ©1997-98 Joe Rivera Jr.

Joe Rivera Jr.
1001 Pine St. #503
• Philadelphia, PA 19107
215-627-2269
joe@jrivera.com

RSVP Callback
answering service
718-857-9267

• (il-u-stray-shon) a
comparison or
example intended
to make clear or
comprehensible,
or to remove
obscurity.

[digital illustration starts here]

• w w w . j r i v e r a . c o m

• (dij-i-tal) data
represented as a
series of digits or
other discreet
forms.

Pink Slip Blues ©1997-98 Joe Rivera Jr.

SAM RASIOTIS

716.594.8147
sxr4517@rit.edu

28 Baylor Circle
Rochester, NY 14624

Nicolás Uribe Benninghoff
RSVP Callback answering service (718) 857-9267

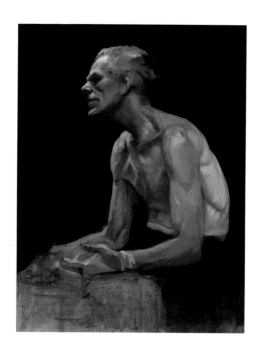

Nicolás Uribe Benninghoff

RSVP Callback answering service (718) 857-9267

Brian D. Martin
Illustration/Painting

2578 Melloney Lane Indiana, PA 15701 (724)349-02█

Liz Lomax

914 · 666 · 7345

CHRISTIAN PANIAGUA

ILLUSTRATION

266 WASHINGTON AVE APT C 14 BROOKLYN N.Y. 11205 (718) 789-4602
RSVP CALLBACK ANSWERING SERVICE (718) 857-9267

zachary pullen
ILLUSTRATION

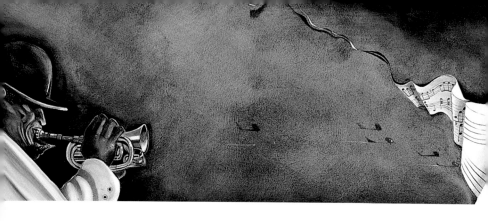

DANA S. JOHNSTONE
RSVP CALLBACK ANSWERING SERVICE (718) 857-9267

GREGSwearingen

1 - 8 0 0 - 2 1 0 - 8 2 3 6 - 0 2

RSVP Callback Service 7 1 8 - 8 5 7 - 9 2 6 7

K. BENNETT CHAVEZ

860-434-8838 RSVP CALLBACK 718-857-9267

K. BENNETT CHAVEZ

860-434-8838 RSVP CALLBACK 718-857-9267

Marilena Perilli

determine me

1628 Library Avenue Bronx, NY 10465 718.823.7023
RSVP Callback answering service 718.857.9267

MIKE ROLL
(A.K.A.) the MIKER
ILLUSTRATOR

9874 FORD RD.
YPSILANTI, MI 48198

PHONE/FAX #:
(734)485-3517

R.S.V.P. CALLBACK
ANSWERING SERVICE
(718)857-9267

PHONE **718.533.0944**

JARVIS

FAX **718.429.5622**
EMAIL **mjjarvis@hotmail.com**

JOE MILES ILLUSTRATION
BROOKLYN, NY (718) 599-2288
RSVP CALLBACK (718) 857-9267

illustration and design

Brian M. Zoll

517.627.6016

RSVP CALL BACK   718.857.9267

DESIGN

tom white.images • *phone* **212.866.784**

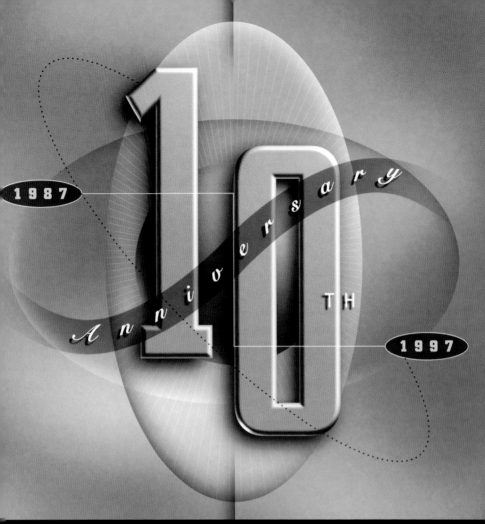

1987 · Anniversary · TH · 1997

website interactive portfolio **http://www.twimages.com** ·

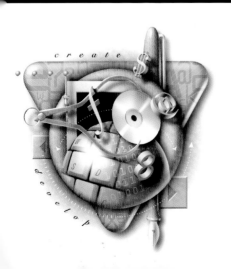

233

Toronto Blue Jays - "Syracuse Sky Chiefs"
Art Director : Tom Collins / Russell Associates

Pontiac / Art Director :Dawn White / Clarion Marketing

Coors / Art Director :Jennifer Highfield / Integer Group

Pizza Hut /MacGregor / Art Director : Mike Pacelli / TLP

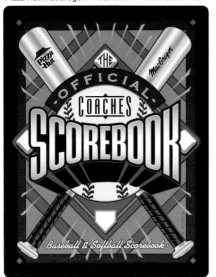

Outdoor Life Magazine / Art Director : Frank Rothmann

TOM NIKOSEY DESIGN & ILLUSTRATION
818.704.9993 FAX 818.704.9995
E.MAIL Logoten@aol.com & nikoseydes@earthlink.net

Windows Magazine / Art Director : Doug Adams

NBA Properties / Art Director : Tom O'Grady

NBA Properties,Inc.

Indiana Tourist Board / Art Director : Michael Harlow / Bates USA

Mori Pro Records - Japan / Joey Carbone : Producer

TCI Cable / Art Director : David Shiedt / Thomas & Perkins

TOM NIKOSEY DESIGN & ILLUSTRATION
818.704.9993 FAX 818.704.9995
E.MAIL Logoten@aol.com & nikoseydes@earthlink.net

Client: New York City Road Runners Club

Client: ESPN/KS&E

Client: KS&E/City of New York

Client: Arthur Ashe Institute for Urban Health

Client: PSP/Nokia

Client: Silver Star Production (Broadway Musical)

Dan Giella ▪ 212.255.8627 ▪ www.dangiella.com

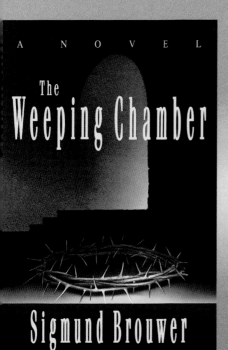

A NOVEL

The
Weeping Chamber

Sigmund Brouwer

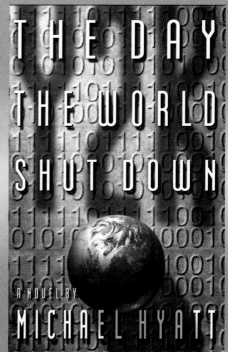

THE DAY
THE WORLD
SHUT DOWN

A NOVEL BY
MICHAEL HYATT

CONTRARIAN INVESTMENT STRATEGIES:
The Next Generation

BEAT
THE MARKET
BY GOING
AGAINST THE
CROWD

DAVID DREMAN
Author of CONTRARIAN INVESTMENT STRATEGY

BRIGHT
STAR

ROBERT LOUIS
STEVENSON III

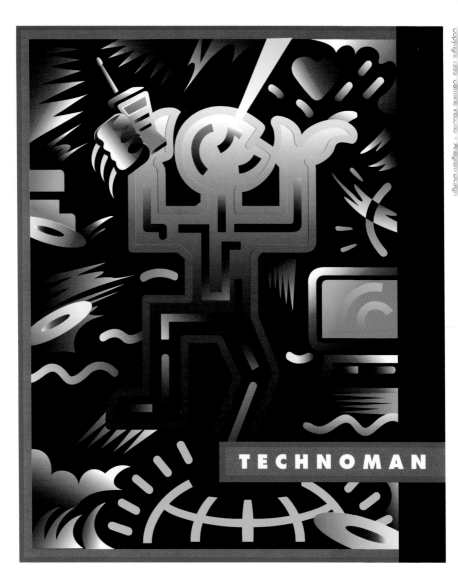

TECHNOMAN

► LOGOS,
LETTERING,
DESIGN AND
ILLUSTRATION.
TASTFULLY
CONCEIVED,
METICULOUSLY
CRAFTED.

CARMINE VECCHIO • ANAGRAM DESIGN • 860 627-6786

CARMINE VECCHIO • ANAGRAM DESIGN • 860 627-6786

Twinings'

Tea Guide

for Connoisseurs

Illustrations from the Twining Teapot Gallery as found at the Norwich Castle Museum, Norwich, England

American International Resources

ESSEX EDUCATION

Nutriceutical Resources

DAVID M. OSHEROW, D.D.S.
ORTHODONTICS

BODKIN DESIGN GROUP

H. ERIC JORDAN
GRAPHIC DESIGN AND ILLUSTRATION
PH (423) 847-6680

ILLUSTRATION

RICK GEARY
CARTOONIST / ILLUSTRATOR
(619) 234-0514
FAX: (619) 231-9035

TATE NATION

843 • 884 • 9911

Doug Rugh

DANA MARDAGA

DIGITAL, TRADITIONAL, COLOR,
BLACK AND WHITE ILLUSTRATIONS

RSVP CALLBACK ANSWERING SERVICE 718-857-9267
888-476-7786 • ADDITIONAL SAMPLES IN AMERICAN SHOWCASE 20 AND 21

barbara KELLEY
corporate portraits/illustration
516 754 7374

VAN HOWELL
516-288-2688

John B
from *Civil War Po*

B
Lawye
from New York Daily
Sunday Book Re

VAN HOWELL
516-288-2688

Above and left:
Hamptons Film Festival

Rightt:
Gen. Edward McCook
Civil War Portraits

See also:
Graphic Artists Guild
Directory of Illustration #15
and previous editions of
RSVP (#13-to #23)

LIZA PAPI

E-mail: lizapapi@interport.net
231 West 25th St. # 3D • New York, NY 10001 • 212.627.7438
R.S.V.P. Call Back Answering Service 718.857.9267

GERRY GERSTEN

THE COOPER UNION

RVEY KAHN 212 752 8490   201 467 0223
FAX 201 467 5905

EMMA CRAWFORD
Graphic Illustration & Design
212.343.7080   908.497.1073

KEVIN
SPROULS

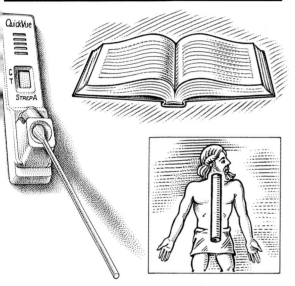

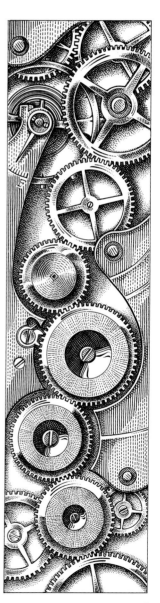

LAURIE HARDEN · ILLUSTRATOR

LAURIE HARDEN, 121 BANTA LANE, BOONTON, NJ 07005 (973) 335-4578

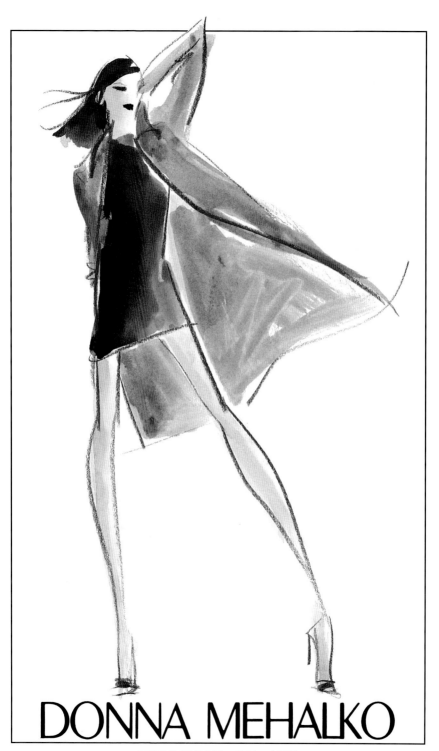

DONNA MEHALKO

PHONE/FAX 212 • 794 • 6297

Richard Lebenson

253 WASHINGTON AVENUE, BROOKLYN, N.Y. 11205 (718) 857-9267

Richard Lebenson
253 WASHINGTON AVENUE, BROOKLYN, N.Y. 11205 (718) 857-9267

"THE CHAMBER" BY MICHAEL DUBISCH

"WE'VE GOT RHINOS" BY C. WATSON DUBISCH

Fantastic Visions Studio
(914) 626-4386
15 SIEBER RD. KERHONKSON, NY 12446

Revelation Studios 415.551.1023
Email: Bigcrunch3@aol.com

George Schmidt

183 STEUBEN STREET, BROOKLYN, N.Y. 11205 (718) 857–1837

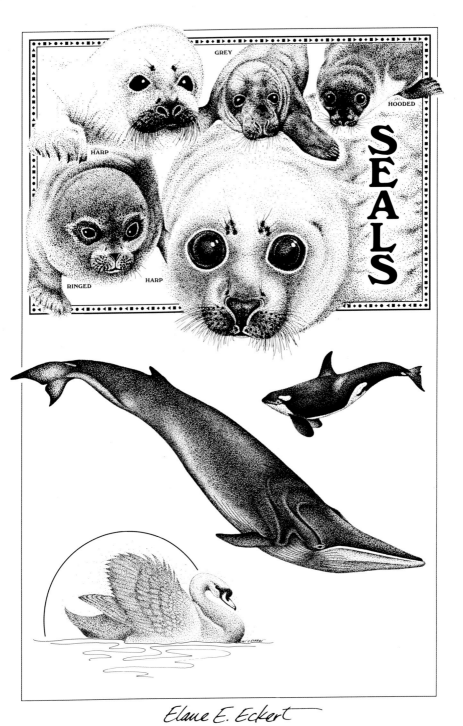

SEALS

GREY
HOODED
HARP
RINGED   HARP

Elane E. Eckert
516.423.0851
556 McKINLEY TERRACE • CENTERPORT, NY 11721

Abe Gurvin Festive Illustrations (949)499•200

"Here, Winston—'Prunellidae: a small, sparrowlike bird with inconspicuous plumage, found in Europe and Asia.'"

CARTOONS and HUMOROUS ILLUSTRATION
by DOUG ADAMS   516.879.4577

ADVERTISING • MARKETING • EDITORIAL • PROMOTION

ALL ART IS SCANNED AT HIGH-RES AND SUPPLIED ON DISK OR VIA E-MAIL.

KATE McKEON

Phone: (815) 477-8518
E-Mail: mkmckeon@mc.net

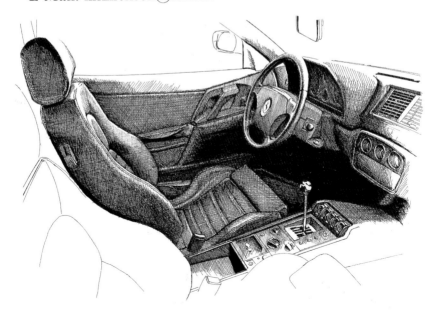

718.788.3709

Illustration & Design · 559 10th Street #3 · Brooklyn, NY 11215

SUSAN DETRICH · ILLUSTRATION

253 BALTIC STREET • BROOKLYN NEW YORK 11201 • 718-237-9174

MORE SAMPLES: RSVP 16•17•18•19•20•21•22•23 • CREATIVE ILLUSTRATION BOOK 1991

GAG DIRECTORY OF ILLUSTRATION 5•6•8•9•10•15 & AMERICAN SHOWCASE 18•19

Monica Gesue
Spot Art, Icons & Digital Illustration

Monica Gesue / Rinkiedink Productions
105 Duane Street, Penthouse C, New York, NY 10007
phone: **(212) 227-8181** eMail: **rinkiedink@aol.com** portfolio: **www.rinkiedink.com**
Clients include PaperMoon Graphics, Good Housekeeping, Disney, Fox Family, Twist, UCLA

JOHN ORLANDO

(516) 872-2626

ILLUSTRATION

STORYBOARDS

DESIGN

Dominick Tucci
<u>Specializing in caricature illustration</u>

26 Tremont Place, Nutley, N.J. 07110 (973) 284 - 0755
RSVP Callback Answering Service: (718) 857 - 9267
e-mail: caricatuci@aol.com

DESIGN

COUNTRYSIDES

Let heaven and nature sing

Culture Shock

if it hadn't been for you!

THEATRE Virginia

SAFARI GEAR

HAPPY NEW YEAR 98

Sunchips

Blessings

PETER·PAN

Feliz Navidad

Michael Clark Design Fax/Phone 804.261.4965
Calligraphy, Lettering and Typographic Design
E-mail typerror@aol.com See www.ideabook.com/michaelclark/

insignia design associates, inc

creative solutions in design and corporate imaging

513.784.1100 • Fax 513.784.0011

**▶ LOGOS, LETTERING,
DESIGN & ILLUSTRATION
TASTFULLY CONCEIVED,
METICULOUSLY CRAFTED.**

CARMINE VECCHIO • ANAGRAM DESIGN • 860 627-6786

Arts

Pizzaz

it aint over!

Breast Care for Life

ZANY

Style

La Forza del Destino

Lenox Hill Hospital

EVANNA

TRISTAN und ISOLDE

Weight

Whistle

Winsor & Newton Artists' Calendar

Wolves

Boston & New York's Smash Hit!

Karen Charatan

K A R E N   C H A R A T A N

phone 201-930-9608   *fax* 201-930-1295

*Handlettering and design
using pens, brushes, and Macintosh computer*

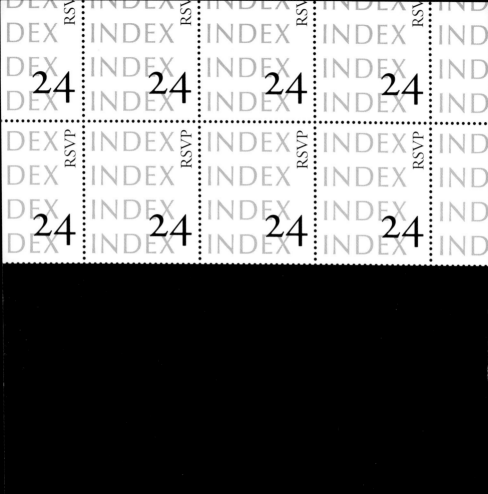

INDEX

ILLUSTRATION

☎ RSVP CallBack Answering Service 718.857.9267

☎ RSVP CallBack Answering Service 718.857.9267

THE LAUNCHING PAD

3D ILLUSTRATION

COLLAGE

SILHOUETTES, PAPER CUTS & CUT-OUTS

WOOD-CUTS/SCRATCHBOARD/PRINTMAKING

CARTOONING/HUMOROUS

☎ RSVP CallBack Answering Service 718.857.9267

CARICATURES

☎ RSVP CallBack Answering Service 718.857.9267

COMPUTER ART

ARTISTS REPRESENTATIVES

FOX ART 213.662.0020   264
HARLIB ASSOC. Joel 312.573.1370 FAX 312.573.1445   103,264
ILLUSION 514.990.2029   193-197
IVY LEAGUE OF ARTISTS/Ivy Mindlin 212.243.1333   167
KAHN Harvey 212.752.8490 201.467.0223   253
LINDGREN & SMITH 212.397.7330   53
MORGAN ASSOC. Vicki 212.475.0440 FAX 212.353.8538   43
NOWAK Wanda 212.535.0438 FAX 212.535.1624   46
RAPP Gerald & Cullen 212.889.3337 FAX 212.889.3341   55
SCOTT Freda 415.398.9121   264
SMITH Averil 610.520.3470 FAX 610.520.3475   198-201
SOLOMON Richard 212.683.1362 FAX 212.683.1919   88,89
TUGEAU Christina 203.438.7307   151-159
TURK Melissa 914.368.8606   167,183-187
WALTERS Gwen 781.235.8658 FAX 781.235.8635   168,169

GRAPHIC DESIGN

ANAGRAM DESIGN 860.627.6786 ☎   238,239,279
BODKIN DESIGN GROUP 203.221.0404   240
CGL MULTIMEDIA CORP. 516.368.2031   58
CLARK DESIGN Michael 804.261.4965.   277
CRAWFORD Emma 212.343.7080 908.497.1073   254
CREIGHTON Kathleen 718.636.1111   71-73
FRISBIE Felicity 718.788.3709   267
HOUSTON Gary 503.248.0510 FAX 248.0245   126
INSIGNIA DESIGN ASSOC. INC. 513.784.1100 FAX 784.0011   278
JORDAN H. Eric 423.847.6680   241
MARDAGA Dana 888.476.7786 ☎   248
NIKOSEY Tom 818.704.9993 FAX 818.704.9995   234,235
ORLANDO John 516.872.2626   270
RIBIK DESIGN Jack 201.641.1456   237
SHAW LETTERING AND DESIGN Paul 212.666.3738 FAX 666.2163   280
VECCHIO Carmine 860.627.6786 ☎   238,239,279
WHITE Tom 212.866.7841   232,233
ZOLL Brian M. 517.627.6016 ☎   228

ART DIRECTION

ANAGRAM DESIGN 860.627.6786 ☎   238,239,279
BODKIN DESIGN GROUP 203.221.0404   240
VECCHIO Carmine 860.627.6786 ☎   238,239,279

LETTERING, LOGOS & CALLIGRAPHY

ANAGRAM DESIGN 860.627.6786 ☎   238,239,279
BODKIN DESIGN GROUP 203.221.0404   240
CGL MULTIMEDIA CORP. 516.368.2031   58
CHARATAN Karen 201.930.9608 FAX 930.1295   281
CLARK DESIGN Michael 804.261.4965   277

☎ RSVP CallBack Answering Service 718.857.9267

GEOGRAPHIC INDEX

SPECTOR Joel (Illus) New Milford, CT 43
TUGEAU Christina (Rep) Ridgefield, CT 151-159
WALTERS Gwen (Rep) Wellesley, MA 168,169

MIDDLE ATLANTIC (DC DE MD NJ NY [exclusive of Greater Metro Area] PA WV)

BUCCELLA Bob & Susan (Illus) Woodlyn, PA 204
CARLSON Sue & Mark (Illus) Waretown, NJ 134
DUBISCH Carolyn Watson (Illus) Kerhonksen, NY 162,260
DUBISCH Michael (Illus) Kerhonksen, NY 163,260
DYEN Don (Illus) Newtown, PA 198
FANTASTIC VISIONS STUDIO (Illus) Kerhonksen, NY 162,163,260
FIKE Denise (Illus) Philadelphia, PA 200
HARDEN Laurie (Illus) Boonton Twp., NJ 154,256
HERGERT Greg (Illus) Pottstown, PA 130
HORNADY Jack (Illus) Washington DC 170
HOWELL, Van (Illus) Westhampton Beach, NY 250,251
LEE Katie (Illus) South Salem, NY 176
LEVINE Lucinda (Illus) Chevy Chase, MD 136
MARTIN Brian D. (Illus) Indiana, PA 216
MAUTERER Erin (Illus) Ocean, NJ 94
O'MALLEY Kevin (Illus) Baltimore, MD 184
PAGANO Peter (Illus) New Providence, NJ 117
RASIOTIS Sam (Illus) Rochester, NY 213
REAM Kristine (Illus) Pittsburgh, PA 106
RIVERA JR. Joe (Illus) Philadelphia, PA 212
ROPER Robert (Illus) Oxford, PA 82,83
SASS Cindy (Illus) Sloatsburg, NY 147
SIMEONE Lauren E. (Illus) Hightstown, NJ 84
SIMON Susan (Illus) Ithaca, NY 156
SMITH Averil (Rep) Bryn Mawr, PA 198-201
SOFO Frank (Illus) East Hampton, NY 157
SPROULS Kevin (Illus) Sweetwater, NJ 255
TORRES Carlos (Illus) Tonawanda, NY 59
TREATNER Meryl (Illus) Maple Glen, PA 152
TURK, Melissa (Rep) Suffern, NY 167,183-187
TWINEM Neecy (Illus) New City, NY 187
WALDMAN Bruce (Illus) Westfield, NJ 74
WALDMAN Neil (Illus) White Plains, NY 86
WHITEHEAD S.B. (Illus) Doylestown, PA 107
ZUCKER Ellen M. (Illus) Philadelphia, PA 110

SOUTH (AL AR FL GA KY LA MS NC OK SC TN TX VA)

AMOSS John (Illus) Decatur, GA 160
BOND Higgins (Illus) Nashville, TN 203
BOTZIS Ka (Illus) Burlington, NC 186
CLARK Michael (Des) Richmond, VA 277
EAGLE Cameron (Illus) Oklahoma City, OK 64,65

MIDWEST (IL IN IA KS MI MO MN NE ND OH SD WI)

WEST (AK AZ CA CO HI ID MT NV NM OR UT WA WY)

The Guild is the only national organization in existence for the sole purpose of making things better for graphic artists.

Join.
Protect your
rights.

www.gag.org

if you talk to your pets for more than an hour, you need to make more friends.

Illustration by Arthur Burdette Frost

join the society of illustrators

We're all fond of our animals, but wouldn't it be nice to have a few lunch buddies with art backgrounds and opposing thumbs?

Illustrators, art directors, educators and those in related fields should be part of this organization and are invited to apply. Contact the Society and ask for membership information.

do it now. before you start barking.

The Society   of Photographers   and Artists   Representatives

The Society of Photographer's and Artist Representatives was founded in 1965 to provide an exchange of ideas and to improve the professions of photographers and artist representation.

For representatives, membership can link you to a coast-to-coast network of the very best in our industry - talent, representatives, and clients - through our monthly lunch forums, our quarterly newsletter, and other publications.

Our membership directory, listing the nations' top reps and their talent, can be an important resource for art buyers or for those seeking representation.

For a brochure of general information about SPAR and it's publications and services, drop us a note on your letterhead. Whether you're a creative interested in working with quality professional or a rep interested in linking up with colleagues, we've got what it takes and we'll give it to you.

SUITE 1166, 60 EAST 42ND STREET NEW YORK, NY 10165   (212) 779-7464

Advertising • Design • Communications

The Art Directors Club, Inc.

An international organization of leading creatives in the fields of advertising, graphic design, interactive media, broadcast design, environmental design, typography, packaging, photography, illustration, and related disciplines.

Gallery located at
250 Park Avenue South(at 20th St)   http://www.adcny.org
TEL 212.674.0500   Email <adcny@interport.net>

THE STARS COME OUT FOR RSVP's DREAMS EXHIBITION

Dreams...Be it heaven or hell, we'd like your spin on this fascinating subject.

So read the call for entries for RSVP's third annual competition. On April 21, 1998, New York's Society of Illustrators saw one of its largest turnouts ever, as the art world came to honor one hundred highly creative interpretations of the dreams theme. Grand Prize Winner Michelle Chang and ninety-nine other finalists and semi-finalists were represented in the exhibition at the Society's Main Gallery. Guests at the upbeat event had high praise for the show's unique concept and the variety of unusual artistic responses it had elicited.

Competition juror Brad Holland talks to first prize winner Michelle Chang, as illustrator Tim Bower listens.

Illustrator Mel Odom and Jackie Merri Meyer, VP Creative Director of Warner Books.

Part of the crowd in the packed Main Gallery.

All photos ©1998 John Milisenda

RSVP Information

Please send me information about

.... appearing in RSVP

.... appearing on the RSVP website.

.... RSVP's next competition

.... Purchasing back editions

.... Purchasing the RSVP Poster Series

.... RSVP Callback®

I am a(n)

.... illustrator

.... designer

.... student

.... other (please specify) ....

Name ....

Company ....

Address ....

City State Zip ....

Phone ....

You can also contact us at

✉ RSVP: The Directory
of Illustration and Design
PO Box 050314
Brooklyn NY 11205

☎ RSVP Callback® 718.857.9267

@ www.RSVPdirectory.com
info@RSVPdirectory.com